Experiencing God's Love as Your Father

Mark DeJesus

Please note the writing style in this book chooses to capitalize certain pronouns in Scripture that refer to God the Father, the Son, and the Holy Spirit, and may differ from other publishing styles. Web Sites that are referenced were up to date at the time of publishing and are not endorsed unless specifically stated so in the writing.

Experiencing God's Love as Your Father

By Mark DeJesus

Turning Hearts Ministries & Transformed You

www.markdejesus.com

Copyright 2018 – Mark DeJesus & Turning Hearts Ministries

Published by: Turning Hearts Ministries

ISBN: 9780692052785

Cover Design: Augusto Silva and 99designs.com

Editorial Assistance Provided by: Stan Doll, Melissa DeJesus

DEDICATION

To every heart. You need the Father's love.

CONTENTS

Your Greatest Need

T he number one struggle Christians often confess to, if they are honest, is feeling disconnected from God's love. They share about a nagging pain of feeling far from Him. Many have never even experienced what close and loving connection with God is like. So when they hear others talk about this subject, it brings up pain within their hearts.

Most know how to talk about God's love or tell others about it, but deep inside, connecting to it for themselves is challenging. This problem has become an epidemic, keeping people from their greatest need in life: *to have an ongoing experience with the love of God in a real and personal way.*

That was my problem. I knew *about* God's love and could tell others about it, but I lacked a personal heart connection to His love for me, especially as my Father in heaven.

> **I did not have a personal and ongoing experience of God's love in my heart.**

So what about you?

Do you experience the love of the Father?

Common, don't lie to me.

And by the way, I didn't ask if you know *about* God's love, nor did I ask if you could quote Scriptures to me. Have you *experienced* His love? Do you possess an authentic awareness of His abiding presence and undying love for you? Does your heart beat with the love Father God has for you? We have to get honest, lest we continue to tolerate a shallow Christian experience, filled with knowledgeable statements, yet void of the power of God's love.

When someone shares that they have a struggle in receiving God's love, it can be really easy to quote a few Scriptures, toss out some pat answers and send them on their way. But nothing will change until a person *encounters* the love of God. The problem is, most Christians are content with a theoretical reference for God's love, with little to no experience of it in their lives.

I knew in theory that God loved me, but that's pretty much where it ended. Yet once I recognized this emptiness and positioned myself for healing, everything changed. I believe the same will occur for you once the wheels of healing get set into motion.

Since that season of heart healing and awakening, I have dedicated my entire life to helping people encounter the power of what the Father's love can do in their life. This is because His love changes everything.

> A personal experience with God's love
> changes everything.

TWO QUESTIONS

When I began to experience the love of Father God in a real way, it revolutionized how I saw myself and my future. When

I moved beyond theory into personal receptivity, my whole world shifted and I entered into a personal renewal.

Before this new awakening in my life, I walked around with two burning questions in my heart that were left unanswered. Most of the time I just ignored them. In fact, throughout my work in helping people over the decades, I have found that all our battles and struggles come down to these two very important questions:

Who am I? *Seeing my unique design and living powerfully from the identity God has given me.*

Am I loved? *Experiencing loving and fruitful relationships with God and others.*

These two questions direct you to the biggest needs of your heart. How you answer them will determine how your life plays out. If you don't get the answers from God and healthy relationships, the enemy will seek to give you convoluted responses that will pollute your heart with lies.

> Your two greatest needs are to know you
> are loved and know who you are.
> Everything in life hinges on it.

"*Am I loved?*" deals with how well you are able to give and receive love in relationships. "*Who am I?*" is all about your ability to live securely from your identity in Christ as Father God's child. On these two foundational precepts, everything in your life is built. Ignore or neglect them and the resulting struggles will eventually catch up to you.

God designed you to be loved. It is also His intent that through experiencing love, you will see how significant you are. Loving connection is meant to empower how you see yourself. Without love, you flounder in life. With it, you gain the confidence to overcome anything.

> ## We must experience love in our hearts.

The thing is, you need to grow and learn what love looks like. As humans, we have to be taught everything we know. Leave most baby animals alone and they can learn to survive with built in instinct. Leave a human baby alone and he or she will die.

You will erode spiritually, emotionally and even physically without love having its work in your life. That is because you were born to know what love is and experience it authentically. You also need the acceptance, validation and empowerment that love delivers.

LOVE MUST BE EXPERIENCED

Most people attempt to engage love by learning more information. The problem is that love surpasses intellectual assent. It cannot be contained by data or formulated on a graph. Love is beyond human computation, for it has to be activated, received and acted on. Love has the power to fulfill the deepest longing of your heart. But you must position yourself to receive, which requires a whole new approach.

Think about someone you love deeply. *Why do you love them? Can you give me the top ten reasons? Is there a formula you can provide to validate your love?*

Although you can attempt to respond to those questions, you will always come up short in providing a complete answer that fully expresses love. At the end of the day, it's something you carry in your heart. There are memories of special moments you've had together and a series of decisions you've made that are a part of this love reference. At the end of the day, love involves the experience of relationship.

> The problem is not knowing about the love of God, but experiencing it in your heart.

Most Christ followers have a knowledge that God loves them. That is not the issue. The problem is the need to connect to His love. We need to move beyond quoting information about God's love and address the problem that so many people feel disconnected from His love. The more we learn about love without experiencing it, the cheaper our reference for love becomes.

Allow yourself the freedom to know that it is God's desire that you *experience* His great love for you. The sacrifice of Christ shows us what His love demonstrates. What Jesus manifested is the greatest example of love ever demonstrated in human history. From that foundation, it is God's intent that His love be displayed to you and through you. Yet it's very challenging to show the Father's great love if you haven't experienced it personally for yourself.

Love Connections

So the next question is, *how do we learn what love is? How do we actually experience love?* The truth is, God originally intended for human relationships to serve as a conduit by which you and I experience love. As you receive and give it out, you actively discover the power of God's love in a real way. God loves you, but you need tangible expressions of love on this planet to give you a reference for what His love looks like.

Earthly relationships are meant to give you a reference and model of the love that God has for each of us. The invisible God chose to make Himself visible through the relationships in your lives. This is where we can have some of our greatest experiences and also our deepest wounds.

> Earthly relationships were designed to give you a reference for what God's love is like.

So what has loved looked like in your relationships? Let's take a look at a few areas where God intended for His love to flow.

UNDERSTANDING YOUR LOVE REFERENCES

Ever had a good friend in life? All your friendships and even acquaintances are meant to show you what God's love is like. Healthy friendships are meant to give you a taste of how God is a friend who will stick closer than even a faithful brother or sister. In fact, Jesus is referred to as our elder brother.

At the same time, I bet you can remember a friendship that didn't work out very well at all. You got hit with betrayal or sudden rejection from a friend that left you in long term pain.

Those wounds can beat down on the life of the heart and leave you with a hopelessness that a true friend can ever exist. Without this being healed, those wounds will be transposed onto God.

Do you remember your first romantic relationship? When you fall in love with that special someone, it is an experience God designed for your enjoyment. At the same time, it is a tangible reference of His passionate love for you.

We all long to experience romance. During the exciting years of courting, it was God's idea for a couple to enjoy the blessing of attraction and romantic pursuit. Throughout this experience, you were made to understand how deeply God pursues you and loves you with consuming fire.

But what about that girlfriend or boyfriend that broke your heart? The guy that cheated on you or the girl that broke up with you out of nowhere can keep your heart wounded and blocked from opening up again. What was meant to be an amazing experience is now a tainted reference. I have witnessed in countless lives, what these unhealed wounds can do to hinder our reception of God's love.

The blessing of love in marriage. The bond of marriage is an opportunity to give and receive the power of committed love. The marriage covenant was designed to help you learn what it means to fully love someone for a lifetime; where you taste of the faithful covenant God has with His people.

Getting married is not just about having a nice life; it is about learning to mature in what committed love means. It also empowers believers to know what it means to be the bride of Christ in awaiting our marriage to King Jesus.

Throughout marriage, you have an opportunity to grow into what it means to love someone unconditionally, the way Christ loves us and gave Himself for us. If you are open to this process, you can learn the power of sacrifice, selflessness, honor and respect in a dynamic way.

But that's not what a lot of people experience. Talk to anyone whose been through the hell of divorce. Maybe you have been through it yourself. For them, covenant love can be a challenging reference. Coldness, constant arguments and infidelity are too often the narrative in many marriages. It often takes a patient healing process to heal from marital wounds. If not, hearts can become embittered and hardened towards the love and goodness that God has to offer.

BLURRED LENS

The fact is that love is so powerful; it can do so much good and empower the hearts of people forever. Yet without it, we are left broken and disempowered. In addition, we develop a blurred lens as to what love is even supposed to look like. This is why we often struggle so much with the love of God. Our relational lens is broken and distorted.

DAD AND MOM

Most of all, our parents are the first and most influential references for how we process love in life. Each time I look at my children with great love, I get another taste of how my Father in heaven feels about me. God's ultimate design is that through your parents, you would get a healthy image of learning and experiencing what the love of Almighty God is like.

Your relationship with your parents follows you all through life. It sets in motion how you see yourself and how you approach relationships. In fact, God meant for your parents to demonstrate what His nature is like. How you hear from God and process who He is has threads of your parent's voices infused into it.

Parents can provide an incredible blessing towards a person's spiritual journey. Yet they can also leave their offspring with deep heartache and emptiness that leave them limping emotionally for decades. The history of too many parental relationships is strewn with great pain and sorrow.

Worst yet, those wounded references get transposed onto God and keep us from the beauty of relating to Him as a loving Father. In fact, if you are honest, you will find that the majority of your struggles in relating to God actually mirror the wounds you carry regarding your earthy parents. Or maybe you aren't ready for that yet. It's ok. Keep reading.

THE SPIRITUAL WAR OVER LOVE

The enemy wants nothing more but to steal, kill and destroy your ability to experience love. If he can break your heart and make you feel separated from love, the domino effect on your life can be colossal. Your diluted perception of love will effect everything else, so the enemy launches most of his attacks on your relationship experiences.

If your earthly relationship experiences dilute your understanding of love, it will then trickle into the lens of how you see God. You may end up doubting God's loving goodness and even consider that He authored those negatives experiences. How we process the wounds in life are critical in how we see God, His love and our connection to Him.

IDENTITY THEFT

The biggest problem with not being connected to God's love is that you won't know who you really are. Because I lacked a heart experience with God's love for me, I struggled for years with insecurity, fear and instability in my identity. I was more comfortable doing things for God than being able to

> Without a revelation of God's love, you will not know who you really are.

receive His love and live from His approval. I lived every day trying to please Him, without realizing He was already proud of me. The enemy knows the quickest way to rob you of your identity is to block your ability to experience God's love.

When you are loved properly, it sets the stage for you to see your identity with an empowered lens. It builds a strong self-esteem and firm security so that an empowered life can manifest. Everything you do flows out of how you see yourself, so it is important to experience a love connection with God, so He can show you who you really are.

On the other hand, if you are not loved properly or feel separated from love, then it can be really challenging to understand who you are. Love is meant to affirm your identity and satisfy your need for validation. Without it, you will attempt to perform in order to find any sense of belonging or security.

The greatest force that a believer carries is to live confidently out of their unique design. Father God's love affirms and calls out who you really are. Without that loving affirmation, you will become prone to hearing who other voices say you are.

Your identity, as God sees it, is not based on performance, achievement or the ability to climb the success ladder. On the contrary, the identity God has given believers is quite simple; so much so that it's easy for many people to miss it.

Your most powerful identity is as a dearly loved child of God. You are sons and daughters. **You are God's child.**

Behold what manner of love the Father has bestowed on us, that we should be called children of God! 1 John 3:1

For as many as are led by the Spirit of God, these are sons of God. Romans 8:14

Identity is very simple, yet incredibly powerful. More than anything else in the world, your central identity is in sonship. He is your Father and you are His kid. The simplicity of this identity is what has been lost over the years.

In fact, I had to revisit this foundations in my life. I needed to relearn what it meant to simply be God's child and live in the security and love of that power. This revelation undergirds our relationship with God for the rest of our lives. Who we see ourselves to be determines what we do and how we will live in this life.

> Your identity is very simple, yet incredibly powerful. You are God's child.

Most of the world has not known healthy love in their lives, so they search the planet for an identity to fill the holes in their heart. They lack a steady security because love has not been firmly planted. When we are connected to love, we won't need to search for an identity; we'll know it and live it out.

Without a personal love relationship with God, we will struggle with our identity. Without a clear identity, we will search for love and meaning in all the wrong places. My search for answers led me to the book of Romans chapter 8, where I experienced a personal revival in the Father's love for me. Out of that explosion in my life, I want to share the power of God's love and His amazing design for who you are. But in order to do that, we need to remove the hindrances that get in the way.

Relationship Interference

There comes a point in time where the pain and emptiness of your heart increases to such a degree that you cannot ignore it any longer. For me, it took an emotional breakdown in my life to realize that I needed healing and transformation in my heart.

During a season of non-stop anxiety and overwhelming depression, my mind was in constant turmoil. I was a pastor in a flourishing church, but was deeply troubled. I scrambled for answers, but soon awakened to what my heart was missing for so long. I knew the information that God loved me in my mind, but did not possess this revelation in my heart.

Like so many I meet today, I lacked a personal reference for God's love. Yet it took me a while to admit this. Even though I had accepted Christ, grew up in the church and was the poster child of religious involvement and service, I lacked an ongoing connection with God's love in my life. To be honest, most of the time, I felt distant and separated from God's love and presence. The more I shared my story, masses of believers confessed the very same heart ache in their own life.

TIME TO GET HONEST

It helped tremendously when I stopped playing games and got honest with God. I simply said, *"Father, I don't know what it's like to experience Your love for me. I don't know how to relate to you as a Father. Can you teach me?"*

I often find that getting real is the best place to start. So if you echo some of these same frustrations, you are in good company. Masses of believers have this same struggle deep in their hearts. Many just haven't gotten honest yet. I had to humble myself and admit my need, so that I could position my heart to be teachable and receive. If I can do it, so can you.

LOVE DISCONNECT

The first thing you need to know about this disconnect is that the problem is not God. I also want you to understand that the problem is not you. Something is in the way, keeping you from being able to experience this great love and live from it daily. We may need to intercept this interference so that love can break through the way it was intended.

> **God does not just have love. He is love.**

Even though it may feel like it at times, God's love for you never changes from day to day. He loves you always, all the time with unending love. Love is who God is. When you experience love, you experience the very essence of His character. God doesn't just have love. He is love. So when you experience Him, love is always there.

So when you feel disconnected to love or God's presence, you must recognize that this is enemy interference. Satan hates the love of God and launches every counteractive agent possible to sabotage your ability to experience love for yourself. He will tarnish your perception of it and give you a counterfeited definition of what love even means.

FEELING SEPARATED

One of satan's biggest assaults against you is to fill you with a sense of separation from God. He does this in how he propagates lies in your thinking. All day long, he is working overtime to keep these destructive thoughts systems in place, so you will continually feel disconnected from God's eternal love.

> The number one symptom of having a rejection mindset is not feeling close to God.

Paul the apostle addressed this in his writing to the Roman believers of his time.

For you did not receive the spirit of bondage again to fear, but you received the Spirit of adoption by whom we cry out, "Abba, Father."

Romans 8:15

There is an admonition here for those who feel distant from God's love: *you have an enemy that seeks to get in the way of love, and it is not you. There is an invisible attack and it is not from God. It is filled with bondage and fear. So be aware of it, because it will seek to prevent you from receiving love and engaging your sonship.*

NAMING THE SEPARATION

This interference creates a mindset that undermines the power of God's love. It is called a *spirit of bondage again to fear*. It is the opposite of the adoption God has sent to us. It is all about rejection.

This bondage again to fear is a rejection mindset.

If you have ever felt far from God's love or felt the need to earn His love, you have heard the lies of rejection. It is the counterfeit to adoption, veiling us from apprehending our identity as sons and daughters and from being immersed in His love. Rejection keeps us bound to fear. It trains us to live as slaves instead of sons. With rejection working in our lives, the potential to receive and live in the Father's love is diluted, blocked and distorted.

Anyone who struggles with landing securely into God's abiding presence will need to expose the lies of a rejection mindset. It is an orphan and slave way of thinking that keeps us from the freedom of being loved as God's child. It even prevents us from being comfortable with who God is as a Father.

THE TWISTED WORLD OF A REJECTION MINDSET

A rejection mindset convinces us that we are not loved and we do not belong. It replays our past hurts to keep us

23

imprisoned, by projecting negative stories onto our life circumstances. It drives us in fear to live a performance driven lifestyle, keeping us from being at peace in who we are.

Rejection trains us to fill the void in our hearts with anything other than God's love. The worst thing about a rejection mindset is that we get used to being rejected and we see so much with an anticipation of rejection. This just scratches the surface on what rejection seeks to do in people's lives.

As I uncovered the brokenness in my own life, I saw how rejection was tied to so many other areas of bondage. In fact, as I began to help other people heal, I saw how just about every struggle that people have is somehow tied to this problematic root. All of this is a result of people not having healthy personal experiences with love.

THE POWER OF ADOPTION

Meanwhile, the power of love and identity is found in receiving the work of adoption.

you received the Spirit of adoption by whom we cry out, "Abba, Father."
Romans 8:15

Adoption bears witness to our spirit that Father God loves us and we are His accepted children. This adoption is a powerful gift, showing us the blessing of living in sonship. It is fascinating to note how Paul used the term "adoption" in writing to the churches in Rome. Under Roman law at the time, adoption was a unique and dynamic process, worthy of observing to help us understand the depth of this passage. It well illustrates our relationship with Father God. Roman adoption was not a mundane thing. It was a significant life event that changed the adopted person's life forever.

There were four powerful exchanges that took place in Roman adoption that are pertinent to our relationship with God today. If you were adopted under Roman law, here are the life changing gifts that would come your way.

1. The adopted person is given a brand-new name.

You would no longer be referred to by your old name. The old identity that went along with your old name would be completely erased as well. With a new name a new identity is given. You don't have to answer to your old name, only by the new. Every time you would hear your new name, it's a reminder of the new identity that you possess.

> A new name is a reminder of a new identity.

2. The old records are completely wiped out.

The legal record of your past is wiped cleaned in every way.

All debts are canceled. Criminal records are erased. It's as if the old person had never been. You are now regarded as a new person entering into a new life, in which the past has nothing to do with you any longer. You now have the privilege of seeing yourself as a member of a new family with a fresh start.

3. The adopted person leaves all rights and connections to the old world and gains all rights as a fully legitimate son or daughter in the new family.

As you enter into this new family, you leave all connections to the old life and the baggage that came with it. Even though you may miss a few things about your old world, what you receive in the new family completely outweighs the old in every way. You have full acceptance and belonging in your new family and the eyes of the law confirms this. No one can dispute it.

4. The adopted person becomes a legitimate heir to the father's estate.

As if it couldn't get any better . . . The newly adopted son or daughter is treated as a complete blood relative in the eyes of the father. You are not only a part of a new family, you have the privileges and blessings that are connected with being a fully legitimate family member.

Even if there were other children who were of blood relationship, it does not matter. The newly adopted son or daughter would join the existing siblings as a rightful heir to all that the father possessed. Who wouldn't love this invitation!

> The enemy does not want you to
> experience the fullness of adoption.

Can we grasp the spiritual blessing involved with receiving the Spirit of adoption? This revelation is what the enemy does not want us to know or experience. When we receive Christ, Father God gives us a new name and a new identity. God the Father is now our Heavenly Father, who has given us a new identity: *sons and daughters.*

With this new family, we have left all connections to the old in order to embrace a new life in relationship with God and His family. We are given a new start, with old records being wiped out so we can freely approach God without shame and guilt. Most of all, we are joint heirs with Jesus Christ.

We are legitimate spiritual heirs to all that Father God has!

> You are not a step-child. You are sons of
> your Father in heaven.

Do you see what is at stake here? Now we can see why there is such a war over people knowing who their Heavenly Father is and receiving His goodness. We are not step-children. We are sons of the Living God!

Not only do we have this identity, we can also have an intimate love relationship with God in the most precious way. This now leads us to the daily experience we can have with God--*to know Him as our Dad.*

Getting to Know Your Dad

W e cannot fully experience God's love without connecting to who He is as a Father. God is a Dad. In fact, despite what has often been misrepresented, God is a really good Dad.

Experiencing God's love must be connected to knowing who He is as your Father. Yet many believers avoid the Father because the word *father* or *dad* is an uncomfortable reference. We wonder why we struggle with love when in reality, the struggle we have is around what *father* means.

> In order to experience God's love, we need to know Him in who He is—a good and loving Father.

The great relationship Christ paid for is that we would know who God is as our Father. This actually became the turning point in my transformational journey. It will become a game changer in your life if you can allow God to heal your perception of what father means.

The entire purpose of spiritual adoption is that you receive the eternal love of the Father in a personal way—to an extent that you relate to Him as *Abba*, as your Dad.

You received the Spirit of Adoption by whom we cry out, "Abba, Father" Romans 8:15

How do we know we have truly received this adoption? The verse gives us the litmus test: *when we are confident in calling out to God as our Dad.* For many, this subject can be very difficult to engage. A swell of awkwardness rises when we consider the idea of addressing God as *Dad*, even though we have biblical jurisdiction to do so.

THE ABBA REVELATION

Abba is a more personal name than just *father*. Father is the formal word, but *Abba* is a more intimate expression. It speaks of *Dad* and can give us a picture of a little child crying out, *Daddy*!

> The message of adoption is to bring you into embracing God as your Dad.

Dad is usually the first word a child says; often babbling and then blurting out *Dadda*! A baby does not cry out *Father* as part of his or her first words; it is almost always *Daddy*! Just as this is an important title to use for a young child, it is eternally significant for us to know how to cry out to our Heavenly Dad.

> God has given you permission to call Him Dad.

Abba is an intimate expression in relating to God, and He gave us the privilege of using it to speak to Him. Yet even

31

though God's Word invites us to call Him *Dad*, there is a real problem with people being comfortable with this dynamic.

I encounter people all the time that get uneasy with the concept of Father God and Dad. It doesn't flow freely through them. Most believers are not even taught about the Spirit of adoption. On top of that, believers around us have not modeled what life can be like when you know you are loved by the Father.

THE DAD REFERENCE

Most Christians understand accepting Jesus Christ for salvation. In fact, most feel comfortable talking to Jesus all day long. But many never take the deeper step of drawing near to the Father. I hear statements like, *"Jesus I am good with. The Holy Spirit I am getting better with. But Father...I don't know where to begin."* This level of intimacy is hard because of the roots of rejection, fear and condemnation that keep them from that freedom.

> Many Christians relate to Jesus well but are uncomfortable with the Father.

Jesus is the way, and His leading is to the Father. Connecting to Jesus is the first step, but without the Father, this is an incomplete relationship. Jesus revealed the heart of the Father and made a way so we could connect to the Father powerfully as our Dad.

In fact, here is what Jesus said about prayer.

And in that day you will ask Me nothing. Most assuredly, I say to you, whatever you ask the Father in My name He will give you. John 16:23

Jesus was saying that as far as petition goes, we need to ask Jesus for nothing. Nothing. It is in Jesus' name that this is all possible, but the request needs to go to the Father. You need to ask Dad.

We have direct access to the Father, in and through the name and person of Jesus Christ. In other words, the fulfillment of what Jesus came to do involves us as sons and daughters having intimacy with the Father. We are sons. He is our Dad.

So why do we ask for Jesus to do things in our lives when He told us to ask Him nothing? In fact, every verse on prayer and calling out to God is directed to the Father. Yet we seem to avoid Him quite often. Listen to most Christian's pray. Most of the time it begins with, "Dear Jesus" or "Lord, please help me..." even though the Bible clearly teaches us to go to the Father.

We don't do this for theological reasons, because the Bible doesn't teach us to pray to Jesus. This habit stems from unhealed brokenness. Our earthly father issues and religious traditions block our understanding of Father God, never mind calling God *Dad*. Let's be honest, it's just uncomfortable and we need some healing.

HEALING THE FATHER REFERENCE

For some, it seems inappropriate or sacrilegious to call God, *Dad*. Approaching Him with that much freedom seems too casual for most. We've never been taught what it means to be safe and comfortable in a relationship with Father God, yet maintain an absolute awe and respect.

> Even though the Bible teaches us to call God Father and Dad, our brokenness keeps us from practicing it.

I know for years as a worship leader, I would never sing the songs that used the word *Dad* in reference to God. I hid my brokenness with religious rhetoric; believing it was borderline blasphemous to call God my Dad.

I am grateful that God began to heal that in me. He was and is incredibly patient and kind in the healing process; always leading me into greater truth without condemning me.

One of the first things He had to heal was my distorted

view of who He is as my Father. Like so many, I was deceived by lies from rejection that kept me from the incredible spiritual strength that comes through knowing Dad intimately.

3 EXAMPLES OF ABBA

Over the years, I have witnessed the tension that arises around this subject. As a result, I always find it helpful to seek out what the Scriptures say, so that we keep our journey built on a solid foundation. In the New Testament, the word *Abba,* is used 3 times. It is found in Galatians, the Gospel of Mark and Romans.

OUT OF SLAVERY AND INTO SONSHIP

And because you are sons, God has sent forth the Spirit of His Son into your hearts, crying out, "Abba, Father!" Galatians 4:6

The Abba relationship has the power to break spiritual slavery off of us while leading us into sonship. Just as in the days of Scripture, we face a tug of war in our hearts, where many are still serving God from a place of slavery, rather than sonship. Their lives are immersed in bondage and religious

---

Abba breaks off spiritual slavery.

---

performance. Slavery has kept them from experiencing the

unconditional love of God, which is never based on our performance. They're living *for* an identity rather than living *from* an identity that is already theirs.

The power of Abba breaks those chains so that we can be free in love and plant our feet firmly into a life of sonship. You are no longer slaves. You are sons.

GAINING ABBA'S STRENGTH

And He said, "Abba, Father, all things are possible for You. Take this cup away from Me; nevertheless, not what I will, but what You will."

Mark 14:36

Jesus Himself cried out to Abba in the most challenging and pressure-filled moment of His life. As He prayed in the garden, His heart was fully aware of the suffering and death that awaited Him. This moment was so agonizing, the Bible says that drops of blood fell from his pores. Clearly, this is one of the most intense moments of His life. He would need the Father's strength now more than ever.

> Jesus called out upon Abba to gain the strength needed to go to the cross.

Throughout His life, Jesus lived in deep communion with

the Father, and it was here in the garden that He needed Abba's strength the most. His disciples fell asleep. His friends were unavailable. Only Dad could provide the kind of strength He needed to move forward.

The cry from the heart of Jesus to the Father was both honest and personal. When Jesus addressed His Father, He did not just use the formal word for Father. He also addressed Him by the intimate expression that a child would use. He cried out to *Abba*, saying, D*ad! I need You!*

> If Jesus needed to cry out to His Dad, then you and I need to as well.

His cry is basically saying, *Dad, if there is another way, please show me. But because You are My Father, I choose to do Your will. And I know that You are with me and will give me the strength to fulfill this.* In His most challenging moment, there was no time for formalities. Jesus needed His Dad.

So do you and I.

In our own struggles and moments of uncertainty, our hearts cry out with a question that says, *Dad, are You gonna be here for me? Are You going to have my back? Will You pull through for me? I need You to show up.*

What do you hear when you ask those questions? Many hear condemning or rejection based thoughts. Worst of all, many hear nothing at all. Our receptors are broken, so we cannot hear His loving reply.

We need to know we can come boldly before the throne of grace and cry out *"Dad, I need you right now"* and be able to connect to His loving power. Because of Christ's example, I can have the honor of busting into heaven's courts as God's child to boldly ask for Him in times of need. But this Abba revelation brings it to an entirely new level. Without this Dad understanding, we will not be able to receive the strength that Jesus carried in His life.

BREAKING FREE FROM REJECTION

Writing to the church in Rome, Paul used Abba to expose a spiritual bondage seeking to block you from a Dad experience with God. Once the love of Abba is received, the lies of the enemy begin to fall like dominos. Dad's love arrives to dismantle those lies and establish each of us into sonship. His love and approval set the foundation in our hearts to walk in a confident and secure identity.

For you did not receive the spirit of bondage again to fear, but you received the Spirit of adoption by whom we cry out, "Abba, Father."
Romans 8:15

Being able to cry out to Dad helps ward off any attempts of

the enemy to implant roots of rejection, fear and insecurity into our lives. This Dad-child relationship builds a strong foundation. It keep us guarded from enemy attacks and enhances our confidence to walk with greater hope and faith.

What a Father Offers

Wherever you have a struggle in connecting to God, it almost always goes back to your earthly father relationship. Whatever frustration or hindrance you carry in your walk with God often leads back to the wound you have regarding your earthly father. Those broken references become transposed onto our spiritual lens and need to be healed.

No matter how great or terrible your earthly father was, you need a deeper experience of what a perfect Father is like. That is who God is.

THE ROLE OF DAD

Dad plays a significant role in our lives; more than people often realize. In today's culture, the importance of a father's influence can get lost, causing us to forget what a powerful father reference looks like.

> Wherever you struggle in connecting to God, it almost always goes back to your earthly father relationship.

Your earthly father was commissioned to help you understand your Heavenly Father. A good dad first establishes loving leadership in the home, where He initiates love with his words and actions. He is called to both speak and show love in the house. His words ought to release affirmation, approval and acceptance. His example helps us to see the nature of God in day to day interactions.

Dad is also meant to be a covering presence. You feel safe around him and receive great comfort, knowing he will protect you. As a spiritual leader, he models a life of integrity and character for others to learn from.

Dad is the first and greatest source of approval for his children. Words like, *"I am proud of you"* or *"I really like who you are"* imbed confidence in the depths of a child's heart. These interactions are so powerful that simple affirmations towards his children can prevent a lifetime of insecurity and emotional instability.

WHAT A GOOD FATHER PROVIDES:

1. Leadership & Mentoring

2. Relationship Initiation

3. A Modeling of Love

4. Affirmation of Identity

5. Confidence & Training

6. Spiritual & Emotional Covering

7. A Life of Integrity & Character

HEALING OUR DAD LENS

No matter how good or bad our earthly fathers were, they all had flaws. The key is that we need to bring the good, the bad and the ugly to our perfect Father in heaven, so He can heal and restore broken places. For many, the image of father needs to be completely reconstructed, because the references are so damaged and toxic. Unless we engage this renovation process, we will continue to avoid Father God.

It becomes hard to relate to Father God as Dad if any of these wounds reflect what our earthly fathers were like:

Dad was unapproachable.

Dad was never around.

Dad abandoned the family.

Dad passed away early.

Dad's time was focused more on work and not the family.

Dad had a really bad anger problem.

Dad was abusive.

Dad was silent and often passive.

When I needed Dad the most, he was not there.

Dad didn't train me for the real world.

Dad was an alcoholic.

Dad only pointed out what I did wrong and not what I did right.

Dad never told me, "I love you."

Dad didn't show me who I was.

Dad didn't pay attention to me.

Whatever statement in the previous list hit you the most is where your God-lens needs to be healed. You often need to experience God the most in the place where your biggest wounds are.

The truth is, our dads only gave what they were personally given by their own fathers. This often shows how little they received. Most of the time, these wounded patterns get passed down from generation to generation, until someone decides to receive healing and change.

WHAT A GOOD DAD OFFERS

If you want to understand what it can be like to relate to Father God in a powerful way, then watch the life of Jesus. He mirrored the Father's heart in everything.[1] In fact, every response of Jesus should help you realize, *"This is what Dad is like."*

---

[1] John 5:19

> When you watch Jesus, it is meant for you to say, "This is what Dad is like."

God is love, and that love was manifested through Jesus Christ. Yet even Jesus had to receive love experiences from Dad so He could give it out. While Jesus was and is God the Word who became flesh, we forget that He lived as a human being. Jesus had to grow up, mature[2] and be filled with the Holy Spirit.[3] He also needed to be empowered with the love and approval of Father God. His example shows what you and I need on a regular basis.

JESUS EXPERIENCES DAD

Before Jesus entered His ministry, water baptism became the initiation ceremony. In the midst of this sacred moment, as Jesus comes out of the water, we see that Father God decides to talk. It is now Dad's turn to say something.

---

[2] Luke 2:52
[3] Acts 10:38

46

> A good father declares his love, affection and approval over his sons and daughters.

It's important to note that there are only three times where we specifically see Father God speak in the record of the Gospels. Two of the three times, we see Him saying what we read here in this account. **This is because a good father makes sure to declare his love, affection and approval over his sons and daughters.**

When all the people were baptized, it came to pass that Jesus also was baptized; and while He prayed, the heaven was opened. And the Holy Spirit descended in bodily form like a dove upon Him, and a voice came from heaven which said, "You are My beloved Son; in You I am well pleased." Luke 3:21-22

With this utterance, the Father of all creation doesn't talk about the majesty of His greatness or His incredible power. He takes this opportunity to boast about His Son. With His words, the Father fulfills three main needs in the heart of Jesus. They are the same needs you and I carry in our hearts today.

Hearing You Are Loved – No matter how strong or tough you may be, everyone needs to hear that they are loved. We especially need to hear it from our parents. Our hearts long to hear the words *"this is my dearly loved son"* or *"this is my dearly loved daughter."*

If Jesus was going to walk confidently and carry the love of God to humanity, He needed that love from the Father to be established in His heart. Notice in this Scripture that love was expressed through spoken words. Jesus needed to *hear* His Father speak love to Him.

You need to HEAR that you are loved.

Many people think that it is not that important to hear that they are loved. But when love is not spoken and expressed to us, it imbeds a reference that says *love does not need to be expressed.* In fact, it can leave your heart empty with no idea as to what is missing.

This is why many will say, *"My parents didn't tell me that they loved me, but I'm good. It didn't affect me."* They end up reproducing the empty references of love they experienced.

Being Affirmed in Your Identity - When the Father said, *"You are My beloved Son,"* He was publicly affirming the sonship of Jesus. He could have affirmed who Jesus was as Messiah or Anointed One, yet He chose to affirm the core identity—Son.

He was and is Father God's *Son*. As evidenced throughout the Gospels, Jesus walked with an immovable security in His

> ## You need to be verbally affirmed in your identity.

identity. He never crumbled or waffled in it. Jesus never doubted His words or actions. He didn't waver in being able to give out love. The Father's declaration sealed validation over the life of Christ. Dad proclaimed His love for His Son and spoke who He was. *This is my dearly loved son!* This identity affirmation imbedded confidence and authority for what was ahead for Jesus.

> ## You need to hear that Dad is proud of you.

The Father's Approval - *In You I am well pleased. I approve Him!* We all needs dad's approval. When a father gives approval to his son or daughter, it's saying, *"I am proud of you! I've got your back!"* We need to hear that Dad is proud of us. I bet if your dad ever told you he was proud of you, the memory of that moment is deeply imbedded in your mind. You remember what he said, how he said it and the circumstances around it. That's because you were designed to know your dad approves of who you are.

We have to remember, in this biblical encounter, Jesus had not begun His public ministry yet. He had not cast out any demons; He didn't heal anyone; His recorded miracles did not take place yet. His ministry had not yet officially begun.

In the Kingdom of God, approval is given at the beginning. The Father gives His approval over us as His children up front. He gives it right away, so that we do not spend our lives trying to earn His approval or seek it from everyone else we meet.

> The Father gives you approval up front, so you don't spend your life trying to earn it or searching for it in all the wrong places.

If Jesus did not receive the foundational approval from His Heavenly Father at the start of His ministry, then He would have been vulnerable to the opinions, approval and demands of people. Being affirmed by the Father gave Him the foundation from that point on to clearly hear what the Father was saying and do what the Father was doing.

The key here is that if Jesus Christ, who lived a sinless and perfect life on this planet, needed His Father's love and approval, you and I as sons and daughters need it too!

> if Jesus Christ needed His Father's love and approval, you and I as sons and daughters need it too!

Yet in order for us for us to experience this love, we will need to address the hindrances that have kept us from it. We will need to get honest and uncover the areas of bondage that have entered as a result of not knowing the Father's love and approval. A major part of this process will involve recognizing where human beings in our lives have not represented the love of God in a healthy way.

Harmful Father Traits

Why do we have such a hard time relating to a good, loving heavenly Father? Because we have no idea what that love and goodness is like. In addition, our pain has left us with so many doubts, fears and baggage that we don't know what to do or where to begin. The solution is love, but our references are blurry and darkened. For too many, what a father is supposed to be has not been demonstrated.

We've all had an upbringing with a father who exhibited one or more of the following traits. You may find that yours is an overlap of these profiles. Here are some harmful father traits that keep you from understanding the Father's love.

The Harsh Father: This type of father may have been friendly, but his oversight of the children was strict and harsh; often riddled with outbursts of anger. The family did not feel safe to make mistakes around him. He may have even been religious or a pastor. He put strict rules and regulations on the home that became more constricting then life giving. His words were more guilt-ridden than loving. In this atmosphere, many began to see God as very moody and angry.

> Someone raised by a harsh father needs the kindness and gentleness of Father God to heal the heart.

The Addict Father: His pain and emptiness propelled him deep into addictions, ranging from alcoholism and drug abuse, to pornography or gambling addictions.

Some addictions were easily seen. Others were hidden in darkness. Yet each vice had a damaging effect on the house. Kids become vulnerable to fear because of the emotional instability that dad had. Their upbringing becomes so twisted that they cannot relate to God in clear and stable ways.

> Those raised by an addict father need to experience the fact that God is a faithful , consistent and honorable Father.

The Performance Based Father: This is the dad who immersed himself into work or activities that involved work-like projects. He was very uncomfortable to simply sit down with his kids and engage heart to heart conversations. He rarely sat still or relaxed--he was always working on something. He was way more comfortable at work and performed well there.

In fact, people at work thought he was great. However, when he came home, he got lost in another work task or home improvement project. In his mind, his way of showing love was through working and doing projects; yet what was really needed was his loving presence *relationally*. His ability to be the loving leader in the home was put on the shelf. He was a slave instead of a son. He evaluated his identity on what he did, not on who he was as a loved child of God.

> Healing from a performance based father involves being loved for who you are as a child of God, not by what you do.

The Passive Father: Passive fathers were often very connected at work but disconnected at home. When he came home, he collapsed onto the couch and was emotionally unavailable. He did not lead the home, which left Mom to do everything around the house, including caring for the kids and doing spiritual activities with them--like prayer or Bible reading. When the family needs his voice, he doesn't step up and speak. He often takes the passive approach to any conflict or problems. Honestly, he hoped most issues would just go away. The problem is, it often left his family in a world of hurt and emotional abandonment.

> Healing from a passive father involves knowing that God is a Father who fights for you.

Absentee Father: This is the father who was never around. He was sucked into work, ministry or removed himself completely. He was absent either physically or emotionally. This pattern runs deep in many family lines. Fathers become overwhelmed with their fears and abandoned the duty as leader of the home to pursue something that allows them to avoid the pain. This abandonment will be detrimental to a child's emotional development and health in the future.

> Healing from an absentee father involves knowing a Father in heaven who will never leave you or forsake you.

The Abusive Father: A father who does not love himself can manifest his internal rage in a myriad of patterns. Those who were raised with an abusive father have experienced a man who has not come to terms with his own brokenness. His words and actions left scars in his children that can take decades to heal. The echo of that pain will linger for quite some time.

All forms of abuse leave intense wounds that keep us from understanding love. It allows the snares of the enemy's strongholds to remain intact. Abuse is not just an offensive act, it can come out of a father's passivity and inactivity in the home. Many abusive fathers had deep pain and areas of mental illness they never dealt with. Their inner pain and torment ended up being taken out on the wife and children.

> Healing from an abusive father takes kindness and patience—relearning what love and safety means for your heart.

The "Make Believe" Father: Everybody wants to feel like they had an amazing father experience. For decades I have had countless conversations with people who clearly had fathers who didn't impart much into their lives. Yet they spoke of him with such glowing praise and admiration that didn't seem to match reality. Everyone else is looking around thinking, *"who are we talking about here?"* To protect ourselves, it's easy to fall into great denial about what we really grew up with.

> Healing from a "make believe" father occurs best when we feel safe to get real with God about our life and history.

The Nice Dad: A dad can be agreeable and civil in the home, yet not activate and equip his children to live as confident sons or daughters. But his dysfunction can be a little harder to detect because he was not overtly harsh, mean or violent. He went about his day and didn't bother anyone. He would often mind his own business and just go along with his daily routines. And that is exactly the problem. He wasn't paying attention to the war his family was facing and the need for him to step up and lead.

> You can heal from what a "nice dad" could not offer without dishonoring him.

THAT IS NOT ME!

In all the cries of woundedness, Father God's heart is saying, *"That is not me! That is not who I am!"* His desire is to let you experience His kindness, patience and nurture. He is not waiting to strike you at any moment. He's not holding your past against you. He is a Father who invites you to sit with Him and connect to His love.

The problem is not God's heart towards us. What we actually need is healing from the misrepresentations of Him that we experienced in our journey. Father God is full of compassion. His mercy is new every day. He is not a moody. He is not distant nor is He passive. He does not determine His love for us by our performance. He loves us and receives us as His own. His desire is that we experience the depth, breadth and height of this amazing love that goes beyond mental assent and connects to the depth of our hearts.

NO NEED TO AVOID HIM

Many people avoid the Father, yet Jesus taught us, when we pray, to say, *"Our Father."* The example of Christ show us what Father connection can be like.

The reason we avoid Father God is because we have a broken heart. Many do not realize they even have a broken heart, yet there are feelings of fear, uncleanness, anger and pain that go very deep. These areas have never been healed.

It can take a while for many to recognize how much their father wounds have had an impact on their life. We often have to go through rounds of denial until we realize the need for heart healing in this area. It is critical for you to know that father wounds can effect everything.

The next chapters will be your opportunity to process the misrepresentations of God's nature you've experienced and dive into what it means to be loved by your Heavenly Father— to know Him as your Dad.

My prayer is that the Father will stretch out His Hand to heal you in the name of His precious Son, Jesus Christ.

Healing the Heart

All healing and transformation flow from the heart. It's the central place of all we hold dear and the core of our existence. It is God's desire to heal your broken heart and fill you with His amazing love. Personal transformation begins with a heart encounter. Yet in order for the heart to engage transformation, the love of God must be experienced in a personal way.

Many reading this will say, as I did years ago, *"I don't have a broken heart. That's only for people that are really, really broken."* Yet recognizing your own personal need for heart healing is going to be critical for every area of your life. Many rush past this issue altogether, while the brokenness of the heart goes underground. We will continue to run in circles until each of us face our own personal brokenness with humility and sobriety.

Unfortunately, the issue of heart healing has been ignored for generations. Most of Christianity saw repeating the sinner's prayer as enough to heal the heart. It produced a lot of shallow and inauthentic Christian living that didn't know how to address problems that stem from our unhealed brokenness.

> ## All transformation begins with healing of the heart.

Healing can begin when we recognize where love has been missing in our lives and address the residual brokenness that has festered as a result. No matter how well we have tried to compensate for that void, each of us has to address our need for true love.

As you listen to the pain and longing of your heart it's important to know that it can only be satisfied by the love of Father God. If this deep need for love is not filled properly, you will continue to flounder and stumble, often filling the void with poor substitutes that do not satisfy or heal.

> We all have to face where love has been missing in our hearts.

WHAT IS A BROKEN HEART?

Heart healing involves having an honest look at our relational experiences that have prevented us from true love and allow God to heal those broken areas. A broken heart is a condition that results from a lack of love in any area of our life. It forms when someone has damaged us or misrepresented what love should be. A broken heart is what leads to the majority of bondage that people fall into.

A broken heart leaves us with a neediness that doesn't seem to get satisfied in life. An unaddressed broken heart can also become hard over time. The pain and heartache of life becomes too much to bear, so walls get put up. Numbness forms. Then people cannot even connect to what's wrong inside.

> A broken heart is a condition that results when we lack love in any area of our life, where someone has damaged us or where love was misrepresented.

Every person on the planet to some degree has a broken heart that needs healing. We also all need a continual filling of God's love. No one can force us to see it; we have to recognize it ourselves.

To put it bluntly, it will be hard for you to move forward unless you recognize that you, yes you, have a broken heart. Therefore, admitting that your heart needs healing in the power of love is a great place to start.

HEALING THE MASCULINE HEART

It can be very difficult for men to address their brokenness. The preconceived notions of what a man is supposed to be, combined with so few mentors have left men floundering in what healing of the heart or dealing with emotions even means.

Most of what is shown today in modern masculinity has nothing to do with being a real man. If superheroes and James

Bond is all we have to offer, the masculine heart is in deep trouble. There is so much more to a man's potential than physical strength and mental toughness.

WHAT IS A REAL MAN?

A real man, is one who lives from an awakened heart—with God and those He interacts with. This heart connection positions himself to represent love in every facet of society, beginning in his home.

Yet the life of the home is where men often struggle the most. They are way more comfortable at work and athletic events, because those are task and performance oriented arenas. A man can hide behind a certain role and keep his walls and masks up. Yet to have a healthy marriage and home life, there takes a lot more heart investment.

Unfortunately, the most uncomfortable place for a man can be in his own house, where He has not been trained to live from a vulnerable and healthy heart. Therefore, most men struggle to lead and connect at home, especially emotionally. They are more comfortable rushing off to work than helping the wife and children navigate through heart issues.

BECOMING VULNERBALE

Many men fear showing their emotions and brokenness. This is understandable, because no one really modeled how to practice that. They also lacked a strong masculine voice that spoke into their heart. Crying, grieving or sadness were seen as signs of weakness and a lack of masculinity.

However, the Bible is filled with real men that were able to show their emotions and vulnerabilities. If we study the life of King David, we find a man that was heart sensitive, yet incredibly masculine at the same time.

> A man of God can weep while also being able to stand up and fight the battles he faces.

David could weep and grieve in the presence of God, while penning some of the most powerful songs of worship. Yet if you were his enemy in a war, he would slice your head off without hesitation. This is a passionate man with a heart that is inclined to God. Connecting to the heart does not strip a man of his masculinity. It empowers him.

PASSIONATE MASCULINITY

I find that Jesus is often misrepresented as a somewhat feminine person—as if He speaks softly to everyone; gives hugs and kisses and tucks everyone in bed at night. Yet there are some biblical examples that show more dimensions of Jesus that also show great masculine passion and fury.

At one time, Jesus was righteously angry over the misuse of selling that was going on at the temple. In a fiery reaction, He not only flipped tables, He made a whip and drove the money changers out. That's a passionate man!

Yet this same man would cry over the city of Jerusalem and the hardness that people carried. He wept over the loss of a friend who just died. Yet this same Jesus showed Himself to John in a vision, where we see fire in His eyes and a sword in His hand. Jesus loves, but you don't wanna mess with this King.

For many men, their masculinity has been stripped, mainly because the investment of fathers has been missing. Therefore, we don't know Father God's heart for us and we lack a sense of knowing who we are as confident men.

CLARIFYING THE CONFUSION

God is doing a strong work to realign what a godly man looks like, according to God's design, not what our broken patterns say. He is in the business of breaking through confusion and building up true masculinity. He is restoring adventure that has been lost in the heart of a man, awakening him to personal passion once again. The chains of passivity are being broken for the men who are willing to let God heal their hearts and build them up.

There is a shaking in the church happening with our precious men. This change is occurring because an unwavering desire to live from an awakened heart is arising. This is so important, because when the heart of a man gets healed and awakened, everybody look out. The world is about to change.

> When the heart of a man gets healed and awakened, everyone look out.

HEALING THE FEMININE HEART

I believe the brokenness in the heart of a man has had a domino effect in the hearts of the women that experienced his woundedness. The majority of a woman's pain can often be traced back to experiences where a man, usually a father, did not represent God's heart to her. He probably didn't know how.

A woman's relationship with her father will form how she will see herself and how she engages her relationships in life. A loving and empowering Father-daughter relationship has the ability to unleash unstoppable security in a woman's heart. As the father invests in the needs of his daughter, he equips her to know her Heavenly Father in a personal way. Meeting the Dad needs of her heart are very critical to her future. In addition to the three needs mentioned earlier, there are important areas to a woman's heart that need to be filled.

To be Noticed - Every woman has a deep desire to know that her father truly notices her; that he is aware of her value and treasures her presence. Just about every day, my daughter will run over to me and show me what she is wearing. Any time she is enjoying an activity, she will immediately call me out to make sure I am paying attention.

> A woman's heart asks her father, "Do you notice me? Do you see me?"

Women who don't get their father's attention can drown under the influence of rejection. She can struggle in feeling like God is not paying attention to her prayers. She can become vulnerable to searching for love and attention in all the wrong places.

To Know She is Beautiful – A father calls out the beauty of his daughter in a way that is pure and empowering. If she does not receive a sense of beauty from her Dad, she will struggle with her self-image and seek to fill that emptiness in unhealthy ways. Receiving the love of Father God and loving herself will become an everyday battle.

Too many women do not see themselves as beautiful, often because they never heard it from their father. When her beauty is not called out, she will search to hear it anywhere she can. It

> When a father calls out a woman's beauty,
> he sets her up to shine with brilliance.

will also give room for the enemy to point out every flaw she has and train her to focus in on them. She'll carry a disgust when she looks in the mirror. Yet when a father confirms his daughter's beauty, he sets her up to shine with brilliance.

To be Protected and Safe – As a protector, dad is responsible for knowing the emotional and spiritual temperature of the home—being aware of the struggles facing each family member.

With that in mind, a good father keeps the wolves away, not by strong arming, but through cultivating an emotionally safe environment. In this his daughter can confidently grow into the woman God designed her to be. Without this safe covering, she can become extremely prone to anxiety, depression and all sorts of unstable mental patterns. On the other hand, a father's protection can allow her to flourish in love.

My wife Melissa and I have spent years helping scores of females experience the healing their hearts cry for. In the process, we have found that the majority of our sisters in Christ do not feel safe. Their battleground surrounds this critical need they were meant to have filled.

To be Treated as a Princess - When you treat a daughter as a princess, she learns how to love herself. As a Dad demonstrates love and affirmation to his daughter, he instills a precious validation in her life.

Please hear my heart: in any of this I am not attempting to bash men. It's simply a call for honest recognition. The broken heartedness of women, coming out of men's inability to love and cherish her, often causes her to marry a passive man that does not cover her. She can also feel the need to be more masculine and shoulder the weight her husband is not carrying.

Yet in the process she can lose the tender love and affection she was so uniquely designed with. If you break a woman's heart, she can lose her powerful ability to love and nurture with dynamic effectiveness.

WHO IS FATHER?

This trail leads us back to what "father" means to you. What kind of patterns and references did he leave in your heart? Did he love and honor you? Did he set you up to know

Father God intimately? Or did he break your heart with his toxicity and passivity?

I ran across this story by an unknown author, which well depicts the power of a father's presence, love and care. Take note to what it does for a this little girl's heart.

A pastor had been on a long flight between church conferences. The first warning of the approaching problems came when the sign on the airplane flashed on: "Fasten Your Seat Belts." Then, after a while, a calm voice said, "We will not be serving the beverages at this time as we are expecting a little turbulence. Please be sure your seat belt is fastened."

As the pastor looked around the aircraft, it became obvious that many of the passengers were becoming apprehensive. Later, the voice on the intercom said, "We are so sorry that we are unable to serve the meal at this time. The turbulence is still ahead of us."

And then the storm broke. The ominous cracks of thunder could be heard even above the roar of the engines. Lightning lit up the darkening skies, and within moments that great plane was like a cork tossed around on a celestial ocean. One moment the airplane was lifted on terrific currents of air; the next, it dropped as if it were about to crash.

The pastor confessed that he shared the discomfort and fear of those around him. He said, "As I looked around the plane, I could see that nearly all the passengers were upset and alarmed. Some were praying. The future seemed ominous and many were wondering if they would make it through the storm."

"Then, I suddenly saw a little girl. Apparently the storm meant

nothing to her. She had tucked her feet beneath her as she sat on her seat; she was reading a book and everything within her small world was calm and orderly." Sometimes she closed her eyes, then she would read again; then she would straighten her legs, but worry and fear were not in her world.

When the plane was being buffeted by the terrible storm when it lurched this way and that, as it rose and fell with frightening severity, when all the adults were scared half to death, that marvelous child was completely composed and unafraid." The minister could hardly believe his eyes.

It was not surprising therefore, that when the plane finally reached its destination and all the passengers were hurrying to disembark, the pastor lingered to speak to the girl whom he had watched for such a long time. Having commented about the storm and the behavior of the plane, he asked why she had not been afraid. The child replied, "Cause my Daddy's the pilot, and he's taking me home."

The next chapter is designed for you to engage the God of creation in personal way—to experience His love and give Him room to transform your life.

We know that God desires to heal you, deliver you, and fill that empty void within your heart. Will it be OK to let him begin that work with you today? For every believer, He wants you to know that you are His beloved child, in whom He is well pleased. Will you allow Him to bring you home today?

Engaging the Father

T his chapter is dedicated to you experiencing the fuller measure of what God's love as your Father can be in your life. It's time for you to begin plowing the soil and setting yourself up for receiving healing.

Let me first encourage you to know that healing is a *process*.

You can certainly delay the process by avoiding it, but you also cannot rush it. Kindness and patience are critical ingredients to heart healing, so give yourself permission to begin a day by day journey.

This section can give you a framework to engage the healing process with more intentionality. In other words, your healing process can have a focus to it. You'll have some questions to think about so that you can begin forward movement into greater healing and love.

Before you begin, place your hand over your heart and ask God to be with you during the healing process. You could start off with a simple prayer:

Father, I want to know you as my Father; as my Dad. I am not sure that I really know what it's like to experience that, but I want to. So be with me as I engage this healing journey. Reveal Yourself to me, that I may experience Your love and healing power in my heart. I give You permission to work in my heart powerfully. In Jesus name, amen.

1. What comes to mind when you hear or think of the words "father" or "dad"?

_____

_____

_____

2. What good blessings did you receive from your father that you can be thankful for? What good things can you celebrate?

_____

_____

_____

_____

3. When you relate to God, are you comfortable relating to Him as your Father? Do you find yourself talking to Jesus more than engaging Dad? What keeps you in that pattern?

_____

_____

_____

_____

4. What areas of your identity do you struggle with? What kind of insecurities and battles do you want to bring to the table? Areas that come about because of a lack of knowing your Father's love for you?

_____

_____

_____

5. Did your earthly father tell you that he loved you? Did he communicate to you that He was proud of you, that you were his dearly loved child? Did he display outward signs of affection? Did you feel special in your father's sight?

_____

_____

How does this make you feel? Be specific

_____

_____

_____

_____

6. Of the harmful father traits, which one(s) were applicable to your earthly father relationship?

_____

_____

_____

6. As you recall memories of your relationship with your father, what kind of wounds do you carry? What needs were not met?

_____

_____

_____

7. What dysfunctional or unhealthy patterns have shown up in your life as a result of this woundedness?

_____

_____

_____

_____

8. In what way, can you forgive your earthly father, for not being what you needed in those areas of your life?

_____

_____

_____

9. What did your father not give you that your heavenly Father can begin to fill you with?

_____

_____

_____

10. In your struggle to connect to Father God's love, what do you find gets in the way? What theme of pain comes up in your heart? *(Abandonment, Being Ignored, God Ignores Me, God's Angry With Me)*

_____

_____

11. Are you ready to make an exchange with God? Now would be a great time to give that wound over to God. Name it out loud and break agreement with it. *(For example, "Father God, I recognize*

that I have abandonment in my life. I break agreement with abandonment today in Jesus name. You are a Father who will never leave me or forsake me. I receive that today.")

12. Take some time to allow God to speak to your heart and fill those places that carried pain and emptiness. Allow your heart to do an exchange with Him, where you give Him those areas of woundedness and receive His healing. Some people like to engage worship music; others stillness. I find that writing can also help.

What do you find that God is speaking to your heart?

_____

_____

_____

_____

_____

13. In what ways can you begin to move forward, knowing that you are loved by your Father in heaven?

_____

_____

_____

_____

I encourage you to connect with someone and begin to share your journey. Allow healthy and safe people to support and encourage you through the process. Keep revisiting the questions and allow God to reveal His heart to love you and heal you.

As an added resource, there are two letters from a father that would be helpful for you to read through and receive in your heart. One letter is written for a son. The other, for a daughter.

I am cheering you on. You are loved.

.

.

A Father's Letter to You

This next section is dedicated to your healing process. Use these letters as a way to gain a fresh lens of what God's love looks like. There are two letters here, one for a son and one for a daughter. I recommend you find a quiet place and place your hand over your heart, so that you can receive best. It's ok to read it quietly, but it can also be helpful to read it out loud. The key is to receive this from your heart.

A Father's Love Letter to His Son

My Dearly Loved Son,

I want you to know that I am so overjoyed to have you as a son. You have brought me such joy by simply being who you are. I am so proud to be your father and I want you to know that I will always be proud of you. From my heart I want you to hear these words, I love you.

With that love, I want you to know that I will be here for you to support, guide and help you in those times when you need advice or simply need an affirming word, reminding you that "you can make it." I want you to always remember throughout your life that, I've got your back and I will be your biggest supporter. You are such a good son, a warrior and a man of God. I believe in you and know you can break through barriers in life.

I want you to know that I deeply desire for you to see the love of God the Father through me. May your heart be filled with the depth of God's love as you receive my love.

God designed you for love and I pray that you always live with His love as your highest priority. May you delve deep into the vast seas of His affection for you by knowing that His love is unconditional and free.

May this love keep you from fear as you realize deep in your heart that God has your life in the palm of His hand. May His sacrificial love remind you to walk free from sin as you daily abide in Christ.

I encourage you to dream big, because you are in the hands of a massive God whose plans are above all you could ask or imagine. The sky is the limit, so be free to reach out for it. I want you to be secure and free to be you and not anyone else. Let God teach you who you are in Him, and don't let anyone form you into a man-made mold that is not a part of God's precious design for you. And while you are living and moving throughout life, know that your Father in Heaven and your Father here on earth are so deeply pleased to call you, my child.

With all my love,

Your Dad

A Father's Love Letter to His Daughter

To My Precious Daughter,

You are an absolute joy to my heart; a special gift that cannot be compared. I am so glad that you were born. I stand in awe of God's goodness, that He brought you into our life!

You will always hold a very precious place in my heart. Not only do I cherish you as my daughter, I am honored to be your father. You are a gift to me. With all my heart I want you to know that I adore you and treasure you as my princess.

You are beautiful and a treasure from heaven. When you walk into the room, I see heaven rejoicing over who you are. I am also so deeply proud of you. Your life is a sign of God's love and goodness.

I want to honor you and communicate the treasure that you are. I want you to hear it regularly from me--may it never get old. I pray that you learn about God's love by experiencing the love that I have for you. I love you so much; and to think, God loves you even more!

God designed you for love and I pray that you always live with His love as your highest priority. May you delve deep into the vast seas of His affection for you by knowing that His love is unconditional and free.

I pray that you see the value in who you are - that you would know you are beautiful and a princess to behold, that you are so precious in my eyes and in God's eyes. You have been ordained for a significant purpose and destiny on this planet. But most of all, I am just deeply honored to have you in my life!

I want you to experience my love in such a way that you will easily know your Heavenly Father. I pray that you receive His love and walk in a passionate relationship with Him all the days of your life. Seeing you serve Him is the dream of my heart.

Know that I am always here for you - to love you, guide you and launch you into your destiny. I will be here for you always. I love you and I will always believe in you.

With all my love,

Your Dad

ABOUT THE AUTHOR

Mark DeJesus has served as an experienced communicator since the 1990s. As a teacher, author, transformational consultant and radio host, Mark is deeply passionate about awakening hearts and equipping people towards personal transformation. He is gifted in helping people address the core issues that become limitations to their God given identity and destiny. He is the author of numerous books and hundreds of teachings. Mark and his wife host a weekly online show called Transformed You and he writes at markdejesus.com. His articles have been featured on sites like CharismaMag.com and Patheos.com. Mark and his wife Melissa enjoy each other and their precious children Maximus and Abigail.

markdejesus.com